Guess Who
Hisses

Sharon Gordon

BENCHMARK BOOKS

MARSHALL CAVENDISH
NEW YORK

Watch your step.

I am in the grass.

I go in the sun to
warm up.

I go in the shade
to cool off.

My body is long and thin.

It has *scales* on it.

When I grow, my skin gets tight.

I *shed* my old skin.

I rub on a rock to get it off.

I do not have legs.

But I am strong.

I push myself across
the ground.

I hide when I am scared.

Sometimes I hiss.

Sometimes I lie still.

I taste and smell with my tongue.

It is long and fast.

The tip is split in two.

My jaws open very wide.

I can eat big animals.

I have eyes.

But I cannot see well.

I do not have ears.

I cannot hear things move.

But I can feel them.

I lay eggs with soft shells.

My babies have an
egg tooth.

It helps them get out
of their eggs.

I like to be alone.

Stay away!

Who am I?

I am a snake!

Who am I?

egg

scales

eye

skin

tongue

Challenge Words

egg tooth
A sharp spot on a baby snake's nose that breaks its egg.

scales
The thin, flat pieces of skin that cover a snake's body.

shed
To lose or fall off.

29

Index

Page numbers in **boldface** are illustrations.

About the Author

Sharon Gordon has written many books for young children. She has always worked as an editor. Sharon and her husband Bruce have three children, Douglas, Katie, and Laura, and one spoiled pooch, Samantha. They live in Midland Park, New Jersey.

With thanks to Nanci Vargus, Ed.D. and
Beth Walker Gambro, reading consultants

Benchmark Books
Marshall Cavendish
99 White Plains Road
Tarrytown, New York 10591-9001
www.marshallcavendish.com

Library of Congress Cataloging-in-Publication Data

Gordon, Sharon.
Guess who hisses / by Sharon Gordon.
p. cm. — (Bookworms: Guess who)
Includes index.
ISBN 0-7614-1767-2
1. Snakes—Juvenile literature. I. Title. II. Series.
QL666.O6G6149 2004
597.96—dc22
2004004230

Photo Research by Anne Burns Images

Cover Photo by *Peter Arnold*/John R. MacGregor

The photographs in this book are used with permission and through the courtesy of:
Animals Animals: pp. 1, 9, 29 (left) Carmela Leszczynski; p. 5 Doug Wechsler; pp. 11, 25
Fred Whitehead; p. 13 E. R. Degginger; pp. 15, 29 (right) Robert Lubeck; p. 27
Breck P. Kent. *David Liebman*: pp. 3, 7, 28 (bottom). *Peter Arnold*: pp. 17, 19, 23,
28 (top l.& r.) James Gerholdt; p. 21 John R. MacGregor.

Series design by Becky Terhune

Printed in China
1 3 5 6 4 2